"With All My Might"

Cochise and the Indian Wars

Arlan Dean

ROSEN CENTRAL
PRIMARY SOURCE™

THE

Published in 2004 by The Rosen Publishing Group, Inc.
29 East 21st Street, New York, NY 10010

Editor: Jennifer Silate
Book Design: Erika Liu
Photo Researcher: Rebecca Anguin-Cohen

Photo Credits: Cover (left), title page, pp. 6, 18, 29   Western History Collection, University of
Oklahoma, cover (right) illustration © Debra Wainwright/The Rosen Publishing Group; p. 10 Denver
Public Library, Western History Collection, A.F. Randall, X-32917; pp. 14, 32 National Archives and
Records Administration; p. 22 The Stapleton Collection/Bridgeman Art Library; p. 30 Private
Collection/The Bridgeman Art Library; p. 31 Arizona Historical Society

First Edition

Library of Congress Cataloging-in-Publication Data

Dean, Arlan.
    "With all my might" : Cochise and the Indian Wars / Arlan Dean.— 1st
    ed.
    p. cm. — (Great moments in American history)
    Summary: A biography of Cochise, the Chiricahua leader, focusing on his
    involvement in the Indian Wars and subsequent peace negotiations.
    ISBN 0-8239-4338-0 (lib. bdg.)
    1. Cochise, Apache chief, d. 1874—Juvenile literature. 2. Chiricahua
    Indians—Biography—Juvenile literature. 3. Chiricahua
    Indians—Wars—Juvenile literature. 4. Apache Indians—Wars,
    1872-1873—Juvenile literature. [1. Cochise, Apache chief, d. 1874. 2.
    Chiricahua Indians—Biography. 3. Apache Indians—Biography. 4.
    Chiricahua Indians—Wars. 5. Apache Indians—Wars. 6. Indians of North
    America—New Mexico—Biography. 7. Kings, queens, rulers, etc.] I.
    Title. II. Series.

E99.C68D43 2004
979.004'972——
                                                                    2003003919

Manufactured in the United States of America

CONTENTS

Preface

*C*ochise was an Apache Indian. He was born around 1810. The Apaches lived in the area of the United States that is now Arizona and New Mexico. Cochise's tribe was called the Chiricahua. The Chiricahua, like other Apaches, moved from place to place to find food and water.

Using mostly bows and arrows, the Apaches were skilled hunters. From the 1830s through the 1850s, the Chiricahua and other Apaches often fought with Mexicans who wanted to control them. During these fights, Cochise became a respected warrior and leader. He also became a lifelong enemy of the Mexicans. There was another threat, however, that was beginning to move into Apache land—white settlers.

In 1846, the Mexican-American War started. The United States won the war in 1848. It took control of what is now Colorado, Utah, California, Nevada, Texas, New Mexico, and Arizona. This included most of the Apache land.

When gold was found in California in 1848, many white settlers started going west to mine. Soldiers were sent to the Apache lands to keep the settlers safe. Soon, fighting broke out between the Apaches and the settlers and soldiers. This fighting was a part of the Indian Wars. The Indian Wars were between Native Americans and white people across North America.

At first, Cochise did not want to fight against the white newcomers. Yet, peace did not last long between Cochise and the settlers. In 1861, a group of Native Americans attacked a farm and took a young boy. Cochise was blamed for taking the boy and he was taken prisoner by a young U.S. Army lieutenant named George Bascom. This event started Cochise's long fight in the Indian Wars. Our story begins eight years later....

This painting is one of only a few of Cochise that exist.
Cochise did not know many white men who would have
painted his likeness or taken his picture.

Chapter One

ATTACK!

I n October 1869, Captain Reuben Bernard led his soldiers into the Chiricahua Mountains, home of Cochise's people. A week earlier, Bernard had been ordered by Lieutenant Colonel Devin to follow Cochise and his people. He wanted Bernard to catch them and kill them if they fought back.

Captain Bernard and his men marched all night following Cochise. Merejildo, Bernard's guide, studied the ground. "Here are fresh tracks, Captain! Cochise is traveling north," he said.

"Very good," Bernard said. "Take five men to the mesa and see if you can find them. I'll lead the rest into the canyon."

Merejildo and his men marched off. Bernard carefully led his men deeper into the canyon.

About halfway into the canyon, Bernard felt a puff of air by his ear. At first, he thought it was only a bug. To his surprise, Bernard saw that the soldier who had been standing next to him was lying on the ground dead—with an arrow in his chest.

"Take cover!" Bernard shouted as he leapt from his horse. Arrows flew at Bernard and his men from every direction.

"Where are they?" a soldier screamed. At that moment, Merejildo and three of his men came running toward Bernard. One man was badly hurt.

"They have the mesa!" Merejildo shouted. "They attacked us before we could get to the top. Jones and Williams are dead."

"All right, I'll take thirty men and go around the mesa from the north. You take the rest to the south. Let's catch him off guard!" Bernard replied.

Cochise looked down at the soldiers marching up the sides of the canyon. He was ready for them. He and his men had control of the mesa. Cochise ordered his braves to stop shooting and let the soldiers get closer. Cochise waited until Bernard and his soldiers were only 100 feet away and ordered his men to open fire.

The soldiers ran for cover as hundreds of arrows rained down on them. They fought back as hard as they could, but it was not enough. Cochise and his men killed many soldiers. Bernard realized that he would need twice as many soldiers to take Cochise and his men. "Pull back, men!" Bernard shouted through the fighting. "Pull back, we aren't going to win this one."

As the sun set that evening, Bernard and his soldiers made their way back down the canyon.

The warriors cheered. "They're gone!" one man yelled.

"They're gone for now," Cochise replied. "But they'll be back. This war is not over." As Cochise and his men returned to their camp, the great warrior thought, *I know the soldiers will come again—but when?*

This photo, taken in 1884, is of Cochise's son, Naiche. Naiche became a Chiricahua chief after his father's death.

Chapter Two

BY THE FIRE

ack at the camp, the Chiricahua warriors celebrated their success over the soldiers by dancing and singing. Cochise did not join in the celebration. Instead, he sat by the fire. His son Naiche sat down next to him. "Why aren't you celebrating, Father?" he asked.

"The white men are everywhere now," Cochise said. "Even here, in our mountains, they come to hunt us. We once traveled these lands, free as the wind. The animals we hunted gave us enough food to eat. Now those animals are hard to find and we must take the white people's cows to keep from going hungry. This is not a good way to live."

Cochise slowly raised his head and stared into the fire. "I cannot forget my brother. Eight years have passed since the white men killed him, but it

seems like yesterday. Do you remember that? You were there, Naiche," he said.

Cochise remembered the horrible events that began his war with the white men. It had all started on February 4, 1861. The sun was setting when he finally arrived at Lieutenant George Bascom's tent, near the Chiricahua Mountains. Cochise had been invited by the young lieutenant. Cochise brought his wife and two young sons along. His brother Coyuntura, two of his nephews, and another warrior also joined him on his trip. They ate dinner with Bascom. Everything was going well until Bascom asked Cochise about a boy who had gone missing.

"Tell me, Cochise, did you or your people take a twelve-year-old boy named Felix Ward from a farm?" asked Bascom.

"I know nothing about that," replied Cochise, surprised at Bascom's question.

"You don't know anything about a bunch of Indians going to a farm and stealing cows and a young boy?" Bascom asked Cochise again.

"I have heard that it was your people who did this."

"Whoever told you that is wrong. My people did not do that," Cochise answered, taking a sip of his coffee. "It may be another tribe. If you give me ten days, I will try to get him back for you."

"Send one of your men to go and find him," Bascom said. "Until then, you and your people will be held prisoners."

Cochise did not wait to see what would happen next. He grabbed a knife he had hidden in his shoe. As fast as he could, Cochise cut a hole in the tent and escaped.

"Shoot him!" Bascom yelled.

Bullets flew past Cochise. One struck him in the leg, but he kept running. Things happened so quickly that as he ran, he still held his coffee cup in his hand. Cochise looked behind him to see who had followed. One of his warriors lay dead outside the tent. None of his family had been able to get away. Only Cochise had been able to escape.

One year after his fateful meeting with Cochise, Lieutenant George Bascom was killed in a battle in New Mexico.

Chapter Three

THE START OF THE WAR

An hour after his escape, Cochise returned to a hill near Bascom's tents. "Bascom!" he shouted. "Let me see my brother!"

Gunfire was the only reply. Bullets cut through the air around Cochise. He raised his fist. "I will get even with you, Bascom!" he yelled. "Indian blood is just as good as white blood."

The next day, Cochise led a band of Apaches to a hill near Bascom's camp. Cochise and three others met with Bascom and three of his men. "Let my family go, Bascom," Cochise said.

"I will not let them go until the Ward boy is returned," Bascom replied.

"I do not have the boy and I do not know where he is," Cochise answered angrily.

At that moment, James Wallace, a stage-coach driver, and two other men tried to reach Bascom and Cochise. Wallace knew some of the Apache language and had worked with Native Americans for many years. He thought he could help to keep peace between the two men. But some of the Apaches that had come with Cochise attacked Wallace and his friends. Wallace was caught, but his friends got away. Cochise and his men turned to run. Bascom immediately ordered his soldiers to fire. Cochise escaped. He now had a white prisoner.

The next day, Cochise tried to talk to Bascom again. He brought Wallace with him. He hoped to trade Wallace for his family, but Bascom refused to trade. Angered, Cochise left. Later that afternoon, Cochise caught three more white men who were riding near his camp. Cochise had Wallace write a note to Bascom telling him that he had more prisoners. Cochise left the note where he thought Bascom would find it. He waited to hear from Bascom, but no word came.

On February 8, Cochise decided that Bascom was not going to return his family. He killed the four white men he held as prisoners. He left their bodies where Bascom could find them.

Ten days later, American soldiers found the bodies. They reported what they saw to Bascom and the other soldiers. Bascom let Cochise's wife and children go, but Cochise's brother, nephews, and three other Apache warriors that the soldiers had caught were hanged. After these deaths, Cochise's fight in the Indian Wars began.

"That was all very long ago," Cochise said to his son. Cochise grew sad at the thought of his brother. They had been very close. "The fighting has not stopped since then. More and more white men are coming to our lands. I do not know how much longer this will go on. I fear we will not always be one step ahead of the white soldiers. Soon, they will catch up."

This photo, taken in 1886, shows an Apache camp in Arizona. When it was time to move, Apache women would break down the camp.

Chapter Four

CAÑADA ALAMOSA

*T*he fighting continued for the next two years. Cochise and his people had to move from camp to camp to keep from being caught. Cochise thought about peace more often. Cochise was nearly sixty years old and he was having health problems. In September, 1871, Cochise went to the Indian agency in Cañada Alamosa, New Mexico.

Orlando Piper, the agent in Cañada Alamosa, heard a knock at his door. When he opened it, he was surprised to see the famous chief Cochise standing there with several of his men. "I have come for peace," Cochise said to Piper. "Many of my people have died. I want to spend the rest of my years here in Cañada Alamosa."

"Please come inside, Cochise," Piper replied. "We can talk in my office."

"No, we can talk out here," Cochise said. His men spread blankets on the ground for the two men to sit on.

"I have many supplies here that you can take back to your people tonight," Piper said.

"My people and I will live several miles to the south. There are about two hundred of us right now. Do you have enough supplies for them?" Cochise asked.

"I have beef, sugar, salt, blankets, and corn. You are welcome to them," Piper said. "Will you be living on the reservation?"

"I will stay where I am camped now. It is a good spot. The soldiers cannot get to us easily there," said Cochise. "In return for giving us supplies, I will keep peace and send out word for other Apache bands to come to the reservations."

It was not long, however, until trouble started again for Cochise and his people.

A reservation was set up in Tularosa, a town northwest of Cañada Alamosa. Piper wanted Cochise to move there in October.

Cochise and many of his people did not want to move. They did not think that Tularosa was as nice as Cañada Alamosa. The grass was dying there, the water was bad, and it was very close to other Native American tribes' lands. Also, the U.S. government wanted to build a fort there, which made Cochise nervous. In spite of Cochise's worries, the U.S. government would not change its decision. Cochise would have to move or soldiers would be sent to Cañada Alamosa to move him. Cochise was very upset that he could not stay where he was. He stopped visiting the agency. He no longer trusted Piper.

On March 30, 1872, just days before he was supposed to go to Tularosa, Cochise disappeared without a trace.

This is a nineteenth-century engraving of General Otis Howard. Howard had fought bravely in the Civil War, losing his right arm. He was very respected. After the Civil War, Howard helped many slaves who were freed.

Chapter Five

A FINAL PEACE

Cochise lived in southern Arizona after he left Cañada Alamosa. His people stole food and supplies from farms and towns near where they lived. Many people were killed during this time. Some Americans wanted to kill Cochise. They did not think he wanted to make peace with them anymore. General Otis Howard wanted to talk with Cochise. He asked Tom Jeffords to take him to the great chief. Jeffords was one of Cochise's only white friends. He agreed and, on September 18, 1872, he set off with Howard and Lieutenant Joseph Slade to find Cochise. They were led by two Chiricahuan guides named Chie and Ponce. Chie was Cochise's nephew.

Over the next several days, the group of men traveled over the mountains looking for Cochise.

On October 1, Cochise arrived at the camp where they had stayed for the night. He got off his horse and hugged Jeffords. Cochise also greeted Howard and Slade. "Why have you come here?" he asked Howard.

Howard told Cochise that he had come for peace. He asked Cochise to move his people to a reservation in Cañada Alamosa. "Why don't you give me Apache Pass?" Cochise asked. Apache Pass had been Cochise's favorite camping site near the Chiricahua Mountains before the white settlers entered the area.

"I think Cañada Alamosa is the better choice, Cochise. There are so many animals there to hunt, the grass is green, and the soil is perfect for planting," Howard replied.

"For eleven years, we have been hunted by the white men. My own brother was killed. I saw his body hanging from a tree. With all my might, I have fought to stop the white men from taking my land and killing my people. Why am I not free to go where I want—like the whites?

If I must live on a reservation, I will live where I am happy. I must talk with the captains of the smaller Chiricahua bands," Cochise said. "It will take ten days for them to get here."

Howard and Slade waited with Cochise for the captains to arrive. On October 10, the last captain rode into the camp. The captains met with Cochise to talk about making peace. When their meeting was over, Cochise said to Howard, "It is agreed, my people and I want to live in peace now."

"If your people agree to live on a reservation," Howard said. "There will be peace."

"We want to live in Apache Pass," Cochise said. "We will not go to Cañada Alamosa." His captains nodded. "If you give us that land, we will not steal or kill anymore. We will stay on our land."

"Fine. That land will be set up as the Chirichaua Reservation in Apache Pass. Your friend, Tom Jeffords, will be made the agent. You will be given food and supplies. However, if you do steal or kill, soldiers will come into the reservation to deal with those who did the crime."

"Very good, we agree," said Cochise. "Tomorrow, we will celebrate."

Cochise's people moved onto the Chiricahua Reservation. Cochise had brought peace to his people, but had agreed only to peace with the Americans. The Chiricahua still fought with the Mexicans, who lived nearby. This angered the American government. In an effort to stop the fighting, the Americans wanted to move Cochise and his people to another reservation in New Mexico. Cochise did not want to go. He did not think that his people had done anything wrong.

Cochise died on June 8, 1874. After his death, the Chiricahua Apaches were lost. Without Cochise to fight for them, the Chiricahua were moved to a new reservation in Florida. Cochise will always be remembered as a great leader who fought bravely for the lives of his people.

GLOSSARY

agency (AY-juhn-see) an office that provides a service to the public

agent (AY-juhnt) someone who works for the government

canyon (KAN-yuhn) a deep, narrow river valley with steep sides

celebrate (SEL-uh-brate) to do something enjoyable on a special occasion, such as having a party

fort (FORT) a building that is strongly built to survive attacks

lieutenant (loo-TEN-uhnt) an officer of low rank in the armed forces

mesa (MAY-suh) a hill or mountain with steep sides and a flat top

prisoner (PRIZ-uhn-ur) any person who has been captured or is held by force

reservation (rez-ur-VAY-shuhn) an area of land set aside by the government for a special purpose

warrior (WOR-ee-ur) a soldier, or someone who is experienced in fighting battles

PRIMARY SOURCES

We learn about history by studying sources, such as old paintings, maps, and letters. People who knew Cochise left plenty of information about him and the times in which he lived. By studying the sources they left behind, we can learn more about Cochise's life.

Writings such as letters give us information on Cochise's dealings with white people. The letter on page 32 was written by H. R. Clum, the man in charge of the U.S. government's Office of Indian Affairs. Clum's letter tells us his point of view of Otis Howard's meeting with Cochise.

Most sources we use to learn about the past tell us their creators' point of view of the subject. By analyzing the painting on page 30, we can identify Frederick Remington's view of a Native American horse raid. Historical primary sources let us see the past through the eyes of the people who were alive at the time. The information these people leave behind helps us understand the people and events of long ago.

Often, Native Americans worked with the U.S. government to capture other Native Americans. This photo shows three Apache scouts and their two Native American prisoners.

During raids, Native Americans often stole horses and cows. This 1888 print by Frederick Remington shows one of Cochise's friends, Geronimo, leading horses after a raid in Mexico.

This photo shows Thomas Jeffords on his ranch. Jeffords is believed to be the only white man that Cochise ever trusted.

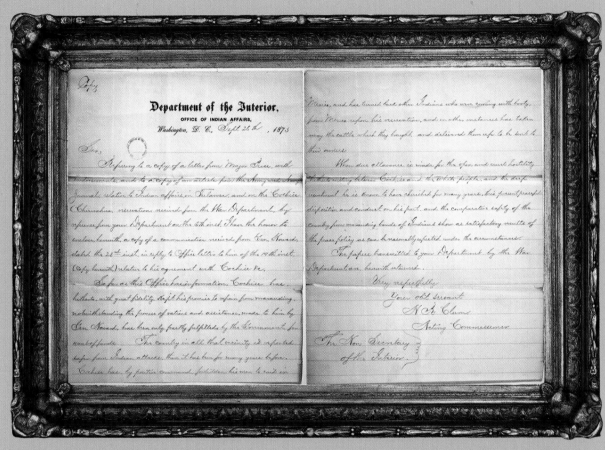

This letter, dated September 26, 1873, is from H. R. Clum, who ran the Office of Indian Affairs. In the letter, Clum describes the agreement between Cochise and Howard. He also writes that Cochise has acted well since the agreement.